STARMAN

The sun is hot, hot, hot – you are driving along a long, long road in the centre of Australia.

Suddenly you see a man standing in the middle of the road. He is wearing an expensive suit and nice shoes, but he doesn't speak – not one word.

You have a gun in your car – what do you do? You must be careful! But you can't leave him here – there is nothing for hundreds of kilometres around – no water or food in this hot, empty place.

But there is something else out there – a very white light in the sky near Wolalonga.

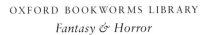

OXFORD BOOKWORMS LIBRARY

Fantasy & Horror

Starman

Starter (250 headwords)

PHILLIP BURROWS AND MARK FOSTER

Starman

OXFORD UNIVERSITY PRESS

OXFORD

UNIVERSITY PRESS

Great Clarendon Street, Oxford OX2 6DP

Oxford University Press is a department of the University of Oxford.
It furthers the University's objective of excellence in research, scholarship,
and education by publishing worldwide in

Oxford New York

Auckland Cape Town Dar es Salaam Hong Kong Karachi
Kuala Lumpur Madrid Melbourne Mexico City Nairobi
New Delhi Shanghai Taipei Toronto

With offices in

Argentina Austria Brazil Chile Czech Republic France Greece
Guatemala Hungary Italy Japan Poland Portugal Singapore
South Korea Switzerland Thailand Turkey Ukraine Vietnam

OXFORD and OXFORD ENGLISH are registered trade marks of
Oxford University Press in the UK and in certain other countries

ISBN: 978 0 19 423427 6

A complete recording of this Bookworms edition of
Starman is available on audio CD. ISBN 978 0 19 423409 2

Printed in China

Word count (main text): 1660

For more information on the Oxford Bookworms Library, visit
www.oup.com/bookworms

CONTENTS

STARMAN

A big red car drives on a long, long road. In the car is a farmer, Bill. He is hot and tired. He wants to go home and have a bath.

Bill listens to the radio in his car and he sings. Bill likes singing. Sometimes people like Bill's singing – but not very often.

The song he is singing is called *Hot, hot, hot*.

There is a sign on the side of the road. Bill reads it: Goondiwindi, 72 kilometres. Dirranbandi 136 kilometres. Bill must drive for a long time. His home is about a hundred kilometres away.

He rubs his eyes. The sun is very hot and the road is long. Bill does not want to go to sleep so he sings some more. A kangaroo hears him and jumps away. Bill laughs, then rubs his eyes again.

Just then Bill sees something. Suddenly he is not tired and he is not laughing. The hair on his head stands up. There is something on the road.

He stops the car and gets out. The thing is a long way in front of Bill. He cannot see what it is – but he does not like it.

Bill gets back in his car and drives slowly. The thing is moving – it is alive.

'What the . . .' Bill says quietly. 'It's a man! What's a man doing here?'

He thinks, 'There must be something wrong.'

Bill stops his car ten metres from the man and looks out.

'Hello,' says Bill. 'Are you OK? Are you looking for something?'

The man does not move or speak. He is looking at the sky and smiling unhappily. Bill looks up too. He can see nothing.

There is a gun in Bill's car. He looks at it. 'I must be careful,' he thinks.

Bill drives five more metres. He can see that the man is about forty years old. He is wearing a good suit – but it is old.

'Hey! Are you OK?' Bill asks again. 'Can I help you?'

The man moves his head slowly to look at Bill. He says nothing then begins to walk. Bill watches him for a minute. He thinks: 'I must do something.'

'Where are you going?' shouts Bill. 'There's nothing on that road. Do you have any water? The sun's very hot. Can you hear me?'

Bill does not know what to do. He cannot leave the man here. 'What is wrong with him?' he thinks. 'Is he ill?'

A lizard runs across the road. A big bird flies near the man. It looks down, hungrily. Near the road are some bones – a dead kangaroo.

Bill is afraid – but he cannot drive away and leave the man.

The man looks very tired so Bill drives two more metres. 'Do you want to die out here?' There is no answer. 'Get in! I'm taking you home,' says Bill.

He opens the car door and gets out. He moves very slowly and talks very quietly. 'It's okay. You can come with me. Get in the car and sit down. I have some water in the car.'

Bill helps the man and he gets into the car. He is very dirty and tired. Bill gives him a drink. The man is thirsty and drinks a lot of water. 'Stop!' says Bill. 'Don't drink all the water. A little now, then more later.'

The car drives fast on the long, straight road. The two men sit and say nothing.

Bill listens to the news on the radio. There is rain in Adelaide. A man in Sydney is 125 years old today. A kangaroo is learning to talk. And a very white light is in the sky near Wolalonga.

Bill likes the news. Next to him, the man sleeps.

Bill looks at him. The man wears an expensive suit and nice shoes. Why is he out here in the sun, without a hat?

They drive for an hour before they get to Bill's house.

Bill leaves the man asleep in the car. He goes into the house and tells his wife, Emily, about the man. Emily always knows what to do. 'We must find out who he is then phone his home,' she says. 'Let's look in his pockets. Perhaps there is something with his name on it.'

Bill and Emily go to the car. They find a wallet in the man's pocket. There is a name – John Phillips – and a telephone number. There is also some money.

'This money is twenty-five years old!' says Bill to Emily. 'Why has he got old money?'

'John Phillips,' says Emily to the man. 'You're very interesting.' John suddenly opens his eyes and looks at her, smiling.

'Can you walk?' Emily asks John. He gets up slowly. 'You're ill. Let's put you into a bed.' Carefully, they help John out of the car.

Bill's dog sees John and is afraid. He runs away and sits under a tree. Bill and Emily help John upstairs and onto a bed. Ten minutes later he is sleeping again.

In the kitchen, Emily says: 'I don't understand this . . . It's not right. He's different . . . It's . . . Oh, I don't know . . .'

'I don't want him in our house. I am afraid of him,' says Bill.

'I know. I'm afraid, too. Let's call the Flying Doctor,' says Emily. 'Then we must talk to his family.'

Bill picks up the telephone and calls the doctor. He tells the doctor about John Phillips. 'I think he's ill. He's very tired and doesn't talk. He doesn't know who he is. Can you come quickly?'

The doctor lives about two hundred kilometres away. He must fly a plane to visit Bill. 'I'm coming now,' he says. 'Look out for me in half an hour.'

Bill puts the phone down. 'Okay. Let me talk to his wife,' says Emily. She takes the phone and calls the number. Somebody answers and Emily talks for a long time.

Bill hears her say: 'But he *is* here . . . No, it *is* John Phillips. We have his wallet – his name is in it . . . Hello! Hello! Are you there? . . . Oh. What? When? . . . I don't understand . . . Okay. Thank you. Goodbye.' When she stops talking, her face is white.

She looks at Bill and says: 'This is all wrong. "John Phillips is missing," his wife says.'

'For how long?' says Bill.

'Thirty years,' says Emily. 'His wife has a new husband now. They have three children!'

The Flying Doctor is late. After an hour he arrives in his plane.

'I'm sorry,' he says. 'This is a new plane – but sometimes it doesn't go very well. I must take it to a mechanic. But it doesn't matter now. I'm here.'

Bill tells him everything. The doctor asks a lot of questions, then goes to see the man. John Phillips is looking at the plane through the window.

'Hello, John,' says the doctor. 'I'm a doctor and I need to ask you some questions. Can you remember your name? Can you remember where you live?' John does not answer.

The doctor talks to Bill and Emily. He says: 'John hasn't got any broken bones . . . but I'm not happy about him. I want to take him to hospital.'

They put John in the plane next to the doctor. 'Phone us,' says Emily when the doctor gets in the plane. 'Phone us from the hospital.' Soon the doctor and John Phillips are high in the sky.

Suddenly John speaks for the first time. He talks slowly: 'I don't want to be here. I want to be with my friends. They are looking for me.'

John stands up in the plane.

'Wait, you can't do that,' says the doctor. 'Sit down!'

John opens the door and says to the doctor: 'You can come too. Do you want to?'

'What?' shouts the doctor.

John looks into the doctor's eyes. The doctor cannot move. He cannot look away. It is cold in the plane but the doctor is hot. John's eyes are looking straight through him.

'Come with me. It's a good place. It's better than here.'

'How can I?' says the doctor quietly. Then John jumps.

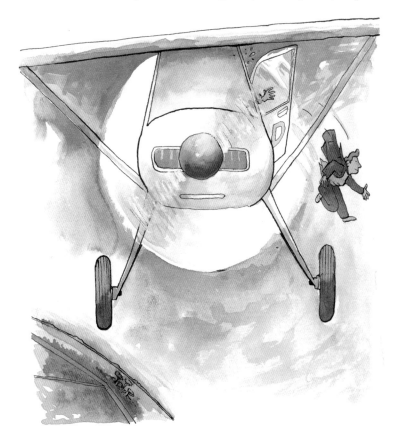

The doctor looks out of the window. John is falling – down, down, down. But the doctor can see a smile on his face.

'He isn't going to die,' thinks the doctor. 'He knows that.'

There are small trees below the plane. Cars drive on a long road. Kangaroos jump all around. John is very small now and he is falling fast.

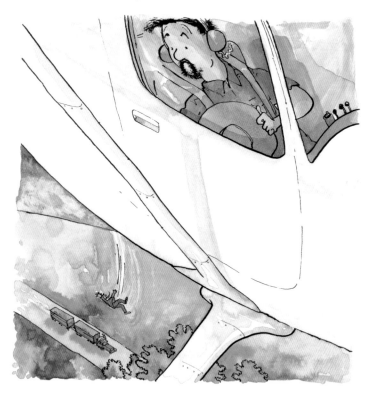

John is twenty metres above the trees. A kangaroo looks up, but John is not falling any more. A beam of light stops him and takes him away. Up, up, up.

The doctor closes his eyes. The light is very, very white. When he opens his eyes the light is not there. John is not there. The doctor sees something in the sky. Then there is nothing.

He is very unhappy – more unhappy than ever. 'I want to go too!' he says.

Roy Cole is a mechanic and he works in an airport. Today he is happy. The sun is nice and warm. Tomorrow is Saturday, and this weekend Roy is buying a new car. He is excited.

He is eating a sandwich when he hears the plane. He looks up and sees it in the sky. The plane is coming to the airport. It gets very near. In the plane, Roy can see a man.

'Who is this?' thinks Roy. 'I don't know this plane.' He puts his sandwich in his pocket.

The plane stops at the airport and a man gets out. Roy
begins to walk across to him.

The man stands still and looks at the sky. There is a
small smile on his face. His suit is dirty and he looks
tired.

'Oh dear!' thinks Roy. 'What's the matter with him?'

Roy likes to talk to people. He smiles, then talks to the
man. 'Perhaps I can help him,' he thinks.

'Hi, I'm Roy. Who are you?' Roy puts his hand out but
the man does not move. Roy puts his hand in his pocket
and looks at the plane.

Roy says to the man, 'Wow! What a wonderful plane. It's more than thirty years old. It's an old Flying Doctor's plane, isn't it?'

Suddenly the man looks at Roy and says: 'Flying Doctor. Yes, that's right. I'm a Flying Doctor.'

'A Flying Doctor? Of course you are,' says Roy with a smile. 'Where do you live? Where do you want to go?'

The doctor begins to get into the plane again. Then he stops and looks into Roy's eyes. Roy hears him say: 'I live a long way away now. I must go back. Do you want to come with me?'

Suddenly Roy feels hot. The doctor's eyes are looking straight through him. 'How can I?' says Roy.

'I can help you. Get in my plane,' says the doctor.

GLOSSARY

bath this is full of water and you can wash in it

broken in more than one piece

doctor a person who works with people who are ill

farmer a person who works on the land

gun you can shoot people with this

hospital a place where you take people who are ill

husband the man who a woman marries

jump to move quickly through the air

mechanic a person who works with machines

missing nobody knows where he or she is

news you read this in the newspaper or watch it on the TV

pocket a place in your shirt or trousers where you can put
    things

rub to move your hands over

shout to speak loudly

song music that you sing

straight in a line

suit trousers and jacket

unhappy not happy

Starman

ACTIVITIES

Before Reading

1 Look at the front and back cover of the book. Now answer these questions.

1 Where does the story happen? Yes No

  a In the mountains. ☐ ☐

  b In the city. ☐ ☐

  c In a hot country. ☐ ☐

2 What sort of book is it?

  a An amusing story. ☐ ☐

  b A love story. ☐ ☐

  c A science fiction story. ☐ ☐

3 A man is lost in the desert. What does he need?

  a A hat. ☐ ☐

  b Some water. ☐ ☐

  c A hair dryer. ☐ ☐

  d Food. ☐ ☐

4 What do you think happens to the man?

  a He dies and a kangaroo eats him. ☐ ☐

  b A farmer rescues him and takes him home. ☐ ☐

  c He finds a horse and rides to a town. ☐ ☐

ACTIVITIES

While Reading

1 Read pages 1–6 and then answer these questions.

1 What song is Bill singing?
2 How far is it from Goondiwindi to Dirranbandi?
3 What does Bill see on page 3?
4 What animal's bones are on page 6?

2 Read pages 7–12 and then answer these questions.

1 What does Bill give to John?
2 How old is the man in Sydney?
3 Put these sentences in the correct order.
  Number them 1-4.
  a ☐ Bill goes in the house.
  b ☐ Bill phones the doctor.
  c ☐ Emily looks in John's pockets.
  d ☐ Bill and Emily help John into bed.
4 How does the Doctor get to his patients?
5 What does the dog do when he sees John?

3 Read pages 13–18. Who says these words?

1 'Okay. Let me talk to his wife.'
2 'This is a new plane – but sometimes it doesn't go very well.'

3 'I want to be with my friends. They are looking for me.'

4 'Phone us from the hospital.'

5 'He isn't going to die.'

4 **Look at pages 19–24 and answer these questions about John.**

1 What colour is his suit?

2 Why is he falling from the plane?

3 Why doesn't he fall to the ground?

5 **Look at pages 19–24 and answer these questions about the doctor.**

1 Why does the Doctor close his eyes on page 19?

2 Where does the Doctor say he lives?

3 What type of Doctor is he?

6 **Look at pages 19–24 and answer these questions about Roy.**

1 Where does he work?

2 Why is he happy on page 20?

3 Why does he feel hot?

After Reading

1 Finish these sentences.

1 John is thirsty because . . .
2 Emily takes John upstairs because . . .
3 John's wife is surprised because . . .
4 The Doctor takes John to hospital because . . .

2 Imagine John meets his wife after thirty years. What does he say to her. Include these words: *desert hot light children home sky afraid friends*

....
....
....
....
....
....
....
....
....
....
....
....

3 Match the beginnings and endings of these sentences.

1 Bill is a farmer and . . .
2 After the plane lands . . .
3 Emily picks up the phone . . .
4 As they drive, John falls asleep . . .
5 John jumps out of the plane . . .

6 . . . but does not hit the ground.
7 . . . because he is very tired.
8 . . . Roy walks towards to the Doctor.
9 . . . and talks to John's wife.
10 . . . he drives a red car.

ABOUT THE AUTHORS

Mark Foster and Phillip Burrows have worked as a writer/illustrator team since 1991. They were born three years and many miles apart, but they are very nearly twins. They drive the same car, work on the same computers, and wear the same wellington boots – but not at the same time! They spend all the money they get from writing on gadgets, but please don't tell their wives. Mark and Phill have worked together on several Bookworms titles, including the two thriller and adventure stories *Taxi of Terror* (Starter) and *Orca* (Starter). When they meet to write, they like to go to expensive hotels, eat chips dipped in coffee, and laugh at their own jokes.

OXFORD BOOKWORMS LIBRARY

Classics • Crime & Mystery • Factfiles • Fantasy & Horror
Human Interest • Playscripts • Thriller & Adventure
True Stories • World Stories

The OXFORD BOOKWORMS LIBRARY provides enjoyable reading in English, with a wide range of classic and modern fiction, non-fiction, and plays. It includes original and adapted texts in seven carefully graded language stages, which take learners from beginner to advanced level. An overview is given on the next pages.

All Stage 1 titles are available as audio recordings, as well as over eighty other titles from Starter to Stage 6. All Starters and many titles at Stages 1 to 4 are specially recommended for younger learners. Every Bookworm is illustrated, and Starters and Factfiles have full-colour illustrations.

The OXFORD BOOKWORMS LIBRARY also offers extensive support. Each book contains an introduction to the story, notes about the author, a glossary, and activities. Additional resources include tests and worksheets, and answers for these and for the activities in the books. There is advice on running a class library, using audio recordings, and the many ways of using Oxford Bookworms in reading programmes. Resource materials are available on the website <www.oup.com/bookworms>.

The *Oxford Bookworms Collection* is a series for advanced learners. It consists of volumes of short stories by well-known authors, both classic and modern. Texts are not abridged or adapted in any way, but carefully selected to be accessible to the advanced student.

You can find details and a full list of titles in the *Oxford Bookworms Library Catalogue* and *Oxford English Language Teaching Catalogues*, and on the website <www.oup.com/bookworms>.

THE OXFORD BOOKWORMS LIBRARY
GRADING AND SAMPLE EXTRACTS

STARTER • 250 HEADWORDS

present simple – present continuous – imperative –
can/cannot, must – going to (future) – simple gerunds …

Her phone is ringing – but where is it?

Sally gets out of bed and looks in her bag. No phone. She looks under the bed. No phone. Then she looks behind the door. There is her phone. Sally picks up her phone and answers it. ***Sally's Phone***

STAGE 1 • 400 HEADWORDS

… past simple – coordination with *and, but, or* –
subordination with *before, after, when, because, so* …

I knew him in Persia. He was a famous builder and I worked with him there. For a time I was his friend, but not for long. When he came to Paris, I came after him – I wanted to watch him. He was a very clever, very dangerous man. ***The Phantom of the Opera***

STAGE 2 • 700 HEADWORDS

… present perfect – *will* (future) – *(don't) have to, must not, could* –
comparison of adjectives – simple *if* clauses – past continuous –
tag questions – *ask/tell* + infinitive …

While I was writing these words in my diary, I decided what to do. I must try to escape. I shall try to get down the wall outside. The window is high above the ground, but I have to try. I shall take some of the gold with me – if I escape, perhaps it will be helpful later. ***Dracula***

… should, may – present perfect continuous – *used to* – past perfect –
causative – relative clauses – indirect statements …

Of course, it was most important that no one should see Colin, Mary, or Dickon entering the secret garden. So Colin gave orders to the gardeners that they must all keep away from that part of the garden in future. ***The Secret Garden***

STAGE 4 • 1400 HEADWORDS

… past perfect continuous – passive (simple forms) –
would conditional clauses – indirect questions –
relatives with *where/when* – gerunds after prepositions/phrases …

I was glad. Now Hyde could not show his face to the world again. If he did, every honest man in London would be proud to report him to the police. ***Dr Jekyll and Mr Hyde***

STAGE 5 • 1800 HEADWORDS

… future continuous – future perfect –
passive (modals, continuous forms) –
would have conditional clauses – modals + perfect infinitive …

If he had spoken Estella's name, I would have hit him. I was so angry with him, and so depressed about my future, that I could not eat the breakfast. Instead I went straight to the old house. ***Great Expectations***

STAGE 6 • 2500 HEADWORDS

… passive (infinitives, gerunds) – advanced modal meanings –
clauses of concession, condition

When I stepped up to the piano, I was confident. It was as if I knew that the prodigy side of me really did exist. And when I started to play, I was so caught up in how lovely I looked that I didn't worry how I would sound. ***The Joy Luck Club***

BOOKWORMS · FANTASY & HORROR · STARTER

New York Café

MICHAEL DEAN

It is the year 2030, and an e-mail message arrives at New York Café: 'I want to help people and make them happy!' But not everybody is happy about the e-mail, and soon the police and the President are very interested in the New York Café.

BOOKWORMS · FANTASY & HORROR · STARTER

Vampire Killer

PAUL SHIPTON

'I am a vampire killer . . . and now I need help,' says Professor Fletcher to Colin. Colin needs a job and he needs money but do vampires exist or is the professor crazy?

Aladdin and the Enchanted Lamp
RETOLD BY JUDITH DEAN

In a city in Arabia there lives a boy called Aladdin. He is poor and often hungry, but one day he finds an old lamp. When he rubs the lamp, smoke comes out of it, and then out of the smoke comes a magical jinnee.

With the jinnee's help, Aladdin is soon rich, with gold and jewels and many fine things. But can he win the love of the Sultan's daughter, the beautiful Princess Badr-al-Budur?

The Omega Files – Short Stories
JENNIFER BASSETT

In EDI (the European Department of Intelligence in Brussels) there are some very secret files – the Omega Files. There are strange, surprising, and sometimes horrible stories in these files, but not many people know about them. You never read about them in the newspapers.

Hawker and Jude know all about the Omega Files, because they work for EDI. They think fast, they move fast, and they learn some very strange things. They go all over the world, asking difficult questions in dangerous places, but they don't always find the answers . . .